Dr. Mark Smith is one those incredible leaders whose personality and presence in any room or meeting exudes the capacity to move teams forward to the best of their abilities. Some participate, others are involved; however, Dr Mark leads, and the great organizations he leads are better for it!

REV. TIM THROCKMORTON
Family Research Council

Dr. Mark Smith understands leadership and has modeled it! I assure you it is not just theory with him. I encourage you to read and reread this book. It has the potential to change your life and destiny!

DR. BENNY TATE
Pastor, 7500 member Rock Springs Church

Leading Above and Beyond is a great devotional read for leaders who desire to be morally above and beyond. Every leader must think and act correctly as they lead!

RICK SANTORUM
Former Pennsylvania Senator and CNN guest

I highly recommend the practical insights on effective leadership that you are about to read. Not only does Dr. Smith do a great job fleshing them out in this book, but he has done an even better job of living them out through his role as the president of Columbia International University.

DR. BILL JONES
Chancellor and former president, Columbia International University

Leading Above and Beyond

LEADING ABOVE AND BEYOND

Making Christ Known Through
the Power of Biblical Leadership

A 30 DAY LEADERSHIP GUIDE

DR. MARK A. SMITH

Columbia International University

Columbia, South Carolina

Leading Above and Beyond:
Making Christ Known Through the Power of Biblical Leadership

Published by Columbia International University
7435 Monticello Rd.; Columbia, SC 29203; www.ciu.edu

Columbia International University exists to train men and women from a biblical
world view to impact the nations with the message of Christ through service in the
marketplace, missions, and the local church.

Editing, cover and interior layout by Kelly Smith, Tallgrass Media.
Cover photo of Yosemite National Park from pxhere.com. Creative Commons (CC0).

Printed in the United States of America
First printing, 2018.

ISBN-13: 978-1-939074-09-6

I dedicate this book to my wife Debbie, sons Doug and Micah, and my daughter-in-law Kierston for loving me while I worked on this project. I dedicate it to the wonderful support team at Columbia International University and to my predecessor, Dr. William H. Jones, for connecting me to CIU. I also dedicate it to the Association of Biblical Higher Education and in particular Hobe Sound Bible College for the huge investment in my life. Most importantly, to God be the glory — great things He has done.

Contents

Foreword

In simple and straightforward language, this brief, readable book gives us biblical principles of leadership from a man who "practices what he preaches." Dr. Mark Smith is a humble servant of the Lord who is not satisfied with "the status quo" but is always striving for "the status go." He's a man who knows what he is talking about. After I finished reading this excellent guide to leadership, I said to myself, "Wow, I wish *I* had read this *before* I began *my* leadership experience!"

The author rightly points out that biblical leadership involves both *who the leader is* (character) and *what the leader does* (competency). Character qualities such as dependence on the Lord, humility, generosity, faithfulness, service, mercy and accountability are underlined as foundational; but added to those are competency skills such as taking risks, thinking big, embracing change, seizing the moment, avoiding short-cuts, overcoming obstacles and critics, casting vision, connecting with others, and training up new, younger leaders. This is a treasure trove of leadership truths.

I am convinced that a prerequisite for *leading* well is first learning how to *follow* well. Mark Smith is a good leader of people, because he seeks to follow the Lord with obedience and great faith. I love his emphasis throughout this book on having a "God-view" about everything he is seeking to be and accomplish as a leader.

So, whether you see yourself as a leader or as a follower, I want to issue a "30-day challenge" to you. Prayerfully immerse yourself in this book for one month (one chapter per day), asking the Lord to make you a better leader. He will!

Dr. George W. Murray
Former President and Chancellor
Columbia International University
Columbia, South Carolina

Acknowledgements

For many years I have written devotionals for my teams. Many of the devotionals originate from life experiences and reflect the lessons that I am learning about life. I have learned to value highly the people who serve so well in the organizations that I have led. Many have helped shape me into the leader that I am today. I appreciate the kind words of encouragement and the ones who have chosen to confront weaknesses in my life. I am a better person because of their words.

There are some who have given their time to contribute, edit and give opinions with regard to this book. I say thank you to all. Debbie Germany has been my wonderful executive who has assisted in so many ways and guarded my schedule for writing. Diane Mull assisted with planning and insights regarding the possibility of this project. Peggy Lee Manoogian was like my right arm, spurring questions, pushing deadlines and gently encouraging, yet keeping me focused when I was tired. Thank you, Peggy Lee! Thank you to editors Greta Clinton, Bob Holmes, Steve Fortosis and Jane Huss.

Last of all, I know that I do not have the ability or talent to write best-selling books — I am nothing unless God works in my life. I acknowledge His help and give Him all the glory.

Introduction

The following incident so profoundly impacted my life that I learned to live above and beyond in this life. This book offers a few of the principles I learned.

That first Sunday in March started as one of the greatest days of my life. I carried my one-year-old son to the car, placed him in the car seat and climbed into our new Ford Taurus with my wife. We journeyed through Indiana's cornfields on our way to the church where I was scheduled to speak that morning. Our conversation reflected hope and gratitude for the blessings of life we had received. After all, I was 30 years old and happily married. We had been blessed with our first son, I was enjoying my first job in higher education, we were planning to buy our first home, and I was only months from finishing my dissertation. We were happy and life seemed just as it should be. After a forty-five-minute drive, we arrived at the church without incident. Part of my message focused on God's sufficient grace for us in times of discouragement. I told the congregation that even in our most difficult situations God will be the sustaining force in our lives. Little did I realize what lay ahead and how true that exhortation was going to be for me personally.

After we shared lunch with a kind church family, I left my wife and son with them while I headed to a board meeting. I got into my car and traveled only about four miles when I was struck head-on by another car. My vehicle spun a number of times and then skidded 120 feet. I was unconscious for a few seconds and then I realized in a semi-conscious state that I was dying. I remember asking someone to please phone my wife. Trapped in the car with smoke billowing all around me, I was suddenly overwhelmed by the thought that I was going to die. In fact, I remember calling out, "Oh God, I am dying!" This was immediately followed by the comforting presence of the Holy Spirit and I knew that while I didn't want to die, I was ready to die.

But my story did not end there. I was pulled from the wreckage and taken to a hospital, where I found that I couldn't walk. This accident placed many obstacles in my path. Here I was — beginning a new career in higher education, about to defend my dissertation in three weeks — and I could not move my left side from the waist down. Everything seemed suddenly to be on hold as I battled for my life.

But with God's grace, I did not give up. The road to recovery was a long and painful journey. It involved many surgeries and three hours of physical therapy every day for a year. I learned to walk again, facing obstacles one at a time and progressing (literally and figuratively) step by step.

I completed and defended my dissertation from my bed. God's grace helped me overcome the challenges in my pathway and changed my world. I have found that His grace is sufficient and He is closer in the times of storm than in the time of peace. My weakness and inability to handle circumstances becomes the occasion for God to more fully demonstrate His strength.

As a result of this event, God showed me how to go above and beyond anything I could ever do before. I read more, studied harder, expanded my horizons, took on bigger challenges, reached for greater vision, and prayed and relied on God more than ever. My God-view changed and I knew my life was destined for service to God wholeheartedly. I have lived a life of total surrender to God for the past 22 years. My life is HIS! My challenge to you is to let Him take you above and beyond in your leadership — it makes life exciting.

*Now to Him who is able to do exceedingly abundantly
above all that we ask or think, according to the power
that works in us, to Him be glory in the church by
Christ Jesus to all generations, forever and ever. Amen.*

Ephesians 3:20-21

Day 1

Leaders Lead with Character

*"A good name is more desirable than great riches;
to be esteemed is better than silver or gold" (Proverbs 22:1).*

The key to success for a leader is character. The world desperately needs great leaders — men and women who will lead the battle for character, virtue and righteousness. We need leaders who will not be distracted by the right or left side of issues we face today, but will focus instead on the right and wrong of the issues. Great leaders are committed to great character. I am talking about who we really are on the inside — at the core of our being. Our character ultimately has everything to do with how successfully we impact the world.

John Quincy Adams said it doesn't matter whether a man is rich; honor and moral character are of more regard. Thomas A'Kempis expressed it this way: "The loftier the building, the deeper must the foundation be laid." Always have something deeper on the inside. Character may be most accurately reflected when no one is looking. But, in the end, I believe it is doing what is right — period. Character matters!

So how does one acquire great character? From a Christian worldview, character begins with accepting Jesus Christ as Savior. Christ is the only One who can transform "characters" into those with godly character. The character journey includes a daily shaping of the mind into the "mind" of Christ. Philippians 2 teaches that, as leaders, we are to take on the humility of a servant as Christ did. Leaders, you are given a great position of authority and power. Do you lead as a servant? Study these characteristics in Philippians 2.

Character requires walking daily according to Christ's teachings on ethics and morality and being guided by a power greater than ourselves: the Holy Spirit. Character is built by faithful, consistent, godly thinking and making right decisions. Do you want to develop character?

Here are some helpful Scripture passages:

"...be transformed by the renewing of your mind" (Romans 12:2)

"Watch over your heart with all diligence" (Proverbs 4:23, NASB).

Leaders, are you developing character so you can lead effectively? The success of your mission may be hindered if it is not guided by virtuous, godly character! You will never amount to more outwardly than you are inwardly.

Be leaders with character.

•

Leaders Experience Transformation

"Therefore, if anyone is in Christ, the new creation has come:
The old has gone, the new is here!" (2 Corinthians 5:17).

During the past several years, I have been privileged to be involved in several sectors of our global world: economic and community development, church work, and education. In every corner, there seems to be confusion and hopelessness as individuals search for life's answers.

It is easy to resort to simple solutions for societal problems when in reality the problems of humanity are much deeper. The fact remains that fallen humanity and sin are the real issues, and only a life-changing experience with Jesus Christ will solve that problem. My family background is a great example.

I was raised in rural Appalachia where only the tough survive. My family did not come from royalty. I had extended family members and friends who fought each other, used moonshine, and lived for the moment. However, the course of history was changed when my grandma met Jesus Christ. Many family members became Christ-followers and everything changed for us.

Leaders, the world needs transformation that comes from Christ's transforming love. Will you lead them to that transformation? Someone once asked Billy Graham, "If Christianity is valid, why is there so much evil in the world?" To this the famous preacher replied, "With so much soap, why are there so many dirty people in the world?" Christianity, like soap, must be personally applied if it is to make a difference in our lives. It is transformational.

Charles Wesley was the 18th child of Samuel and Susanna Wesley. The Wesleys were in London in May of 1738. For a period of time they were staying in the home of some Moravians in Little Britain, not far from St. Paul's Cathedral. As Charles sat listening to the Christian testimonies of his hosts, he was deeply affected. God was dealing with him. Charles said he felt "the Spirit of God striving with his spirit 'till …. He chased away the darkness of my unbelief. I now found myself at peace with God, and rejoiced in hope of loving Christ."

One year following his salvation, Charles wrote a song:

He breaks the power of canceled sin,
He sets the prisoner free;
His blood can make the foulest clean,
His blood availed for me.

Leaders, have you experienced above and beyond transformation?

Day 3

Leaders Begin with Prayer

"I wait quietly before God, for my victory comes from Him" (Psalm 62:1, NLT).

Joshua gives us a pattern for leadership victories in Joshua 5:14-6:21. Joshua prayed, he planned, he prepared, he performed the task, and he celebrated with the people. Read it. It is an awesome story. But first he prayed!

Dr. Parker Palmers says that prayer is intimate oneness with God. Prayer is our communing with God and it involves sharing with and listening to Him. Listening for the voice of God requires quietness and discipline in a fast-paced society with millions of distractions. My father used to ask me, "Did you hear from God today?" A biblical leader spends time each morning asking for wisdom and direction. Part of the leader's prayer life involves leading the organization into a spirit of oneness with the Holy Spirit by asking for new ideas on how to grow and lead. Part of that prayer time may include taking a paper and pen and writing down plans for that day, week, or year. Additional time should be spent asking God for creative ideas. In my life, I have been given many growth ideas during my prayer times. On his face before God, Joshua devised battle plans that are studied to this day. Leaders, do you spend 30-60 minutes weekly thinking about how to lead forward — just creative, Holy-Spirit-led prayer time? It is a secret to leading well.

Here are a few questions to ask in that prayer time:

Lord, where do you want our organization to be in five years?

Lord, how do you want me to personally grow in five years?

Lord, how do we best meet needs in our community?

Lord, what approaches should our team take to accomplish success?

Lord, with whom should I connect to meet needs?

Lord, what will You consider success?

Leaders, I refuse to pray status quo prayers - pray for 'status go.' You were created to make a difference for His glory.

Day 4

Leaders Depend Upon the Holy Spirit

"But you will receive power when the Holy Spirit comes on you;
and you will be my witnesses in Jerusalem, and in all Judea and Samaria,
and to the ends of the earth" (Acts 1:8).

For leaders to impact society, there must be a powerful visitation of the Holy Spirit which radically changes the hearts of men and women toward God. From the prophet Isaiah to Saul on the road to Damascus, the Lord uses transformative experiences to inspire spiritual leaders.

In Isaiah 6, Isaiah experienced a powerful vision of the Lord, which moved him from "Woe is me!" to "Here am I! Send me!" And in Acts 9, Saul goes from a saint killer to a sinner saved by grace!

Over the centuries God has used His Holy Spirit to revitalize entire generations. These generations have acted in His name to influence the world.

Disciples multiply! In China, the average church of 50 produces 500 converts. The American Church was known in its early days for making disciples because of the Holy Spirit's move. What brings about action in a church? Generational action begins when we open our eyes to needs (Mark 3:5), remove our selfish motivations from the equation, and surrender to Christ. This is only accomplished by the Holy Spirit's empowerment, which motivates us to go on the offensive as Caleb did, saying,

> *"Now therefore, give me this mountain of which the LORD spoke in that day" (Joshua 14:12, NKJV).*

What is God calling you to do in your community? First ask yourself, "How has God gifted me to serve others?" Then ask, "What steps am I taking to further His Kingdom?" Then, go and use your God-given talents to evangelize and share Christ. When generational action becomes the focus, mountains are moved by the Holy Spirit's power and influence.

Here are a few questions for your organization:

Are we inviting the Holy Spirit to be present in our meetings?

Who in our organization is working to support prison ministry and is visiting prisoners?

Who is leading an effort to support the widows?

Who is building homes for the homeless and orphans?

Who is feeding the poor?

Who is loving the AIDS victim, the drug addict?

Who is saving babies from abortion by helping a crisis pregnancy center?

Who is leading people to Christ?

True leaders change the world by calling generations to action — yes, even business leaders. It's time to rise up, lead, and act. God is moving in our midst.

Leaders, be strong and courageous, for the Lord our God is with you wherever you go!

Day 5

Leaders Take Risks

"Now to Him who is able to do immeasurably more than all we ask or imagine, according to His power that is at work within us" (Ephesians 3:20).

While reading Joshua, I was also reading *The Circle Maker* by Mark Batterson. This book is very challenging and has been life-changing for me. He says, "The greatest chapters in history always begin with risk, and the same is true with chapters in your life. If you are unwilling to risk everything you will never build a boat like Noah nor get out of the boat like Peter!" Just think, Joshua thought a wall would come down by walking around it! Wow! It actually fell.

So leaders, as you lead your organization, let me ask a couple of questions:

What are you praying for that is so big only God can do it? Will you take that risk?

What one dream for your life or organization is so big that everyone will know only God will be glorified when the dream comes true?

Reading Batterson's book reminds me that God is the multiplier.

5 + 2 = 7 right? No!
5 + 2 = 5,000 fed with a remainder of 12 baskets — I love that multiplier! (Matthew 14:13-21)

So what are you asking God for this day? A new church building to meet needs in your community? A new ministry idea? Five thousand students for a university? Thirty-five students for your Sunday school class? Salvation for 10,000? See, I believe God loves to meet the needs of lost communities.

Don't be afraid to ask. Spiritually mature leaders' prayers are not focused on self but rather on the needs of a community and the world.

Remember the God multiplier: 5 + 2 = 5,000.

Leaders, take risks!

Day 6

Leaders Lead without Fear

"Have not I commanded thee? Be strong and of a good courage; be not afraid, neither be thou dismayed: for the Lord thy God is with thee whithersoever thou goest" (Joshua 1:9, KJV).

Moses is dead and the great leader of Israel must be replaced. Moses has prepared Joshua and the Lord comes to him and says, "Joshua, lead my people!" Leadership transitions are tough. Everyone senses fear. Fear is one of the prevailing factors in the life of a leader that can derail the dream and destroy the vision. Joshua is afraid, but he quickly hears the words, "I the Lord God, I am with you."

Fear causes many leaders not to share vision, enact plans, and reach for the impossible. Yet the same God that was with Joshua is with us. We are reminded in Psalm 145:5 about the Lord, our Creator God. Oh, how right J.B. Phillips was when he wrote the book *Your God is Too Small*. God is infinitely capable of overcoming our fears.

> *"I will meditate on the glorious splendor of Your majesty, and on Your wondrous works" (Psalm 145:5, NKJV).*

Vision must move forward with God's help. Now I understand that we all experience fear. It is a human thing! But I have learned that operating out of fear destroys vision. Reliance on God brings courage. Sometimes we forget Who is in control. After all, He is the Creator God.

Recently, I visited Yosemite. It is 14,000 feet at its highest point with 3,000-foot waterfalls! While standing in awe, my wife said to me, "This makes me want to sing 'How Great Thou Art'." In that moment I understood what Joshua understood. The Creator God is BIG enough! Joshua had a right view of God. He relied on God and had a promise from God that we must adopt.

Leaders, lead on without fear. Take territories for God's kingdom. Do you have a 'Yosemite' God view?

Day 7

Leaders are Generous

"The generous soul will be made rich, and he who waters
will also be watered himself" (Proverbs 11:25, NKJV).

Biblical leaders are generous. Generosity always flows from leaders who love and serve their people. In the Maxwell Study Bible, Dr. John Maxwell suggests that great leaders are givers not takers, and they are motivated to serve in three distinct ways. First, they serve others before themselves. Second, they serve by solving problems, and third, they serve by saving causes. Deuteronomy 15 lays out the plans for generosity among the children of Israel, in which they were asked to release debt every seven years. Do you think that was easy for those who were owed great debts? No, but it reflected God's grace. Models of generosity are found throughout Scripture: Ruth 2 (Boaz and Ruth), Ecclesiastes 11:1-9 (Be generous: invest in acts of charity, MSG), Luke 9:12-17 (In the account of the loaves and fish, Jesus saw a need and tended to it), and Acts 5:1-11 (A negative example in the story of Ananias and Sapphira).

Generosity is a key component of a growing, thriving organization. Do you really want to learn the principle of generosity? Become generous. One of the practices with which I have challenged our team over the years is to practice generosity by giving a twenty-dollar bill on occasion to a stranger in need. This practice requires Holy Spirit discernment but also nurtures a generous heart. Try it this week.

Teaching generosity to family and team members is also important. Our boys will never forget the night we had close friends in our home who were serving in ministry. They were supported by gifts that God's people gave to that ministry. As I had been praying for them, God impressed upon me to ask directly about their financial needs. Debbie and I had saved up $4,000 for household expenses and a new mattress for my bad back (the result of the car accident). When they arrived, I asked my friend, "What do you need right now?" He hesitated but I insisted. He told me their car had blown up and they needed around $4,000 to purchase a used car. I immediately felt the Holy Spirit nudge me to respond, and I wrote them a check.

When one understands generosity, the outflow of being used of God is amazing. I cannot tell you the number of times over the years that God has impressed upon me to violate my budget and trust Him. Every time, without exception, He has provided for us.

Leaders, be generous.

Day 8

Leaders Prepare and Plan

"The plans of the diligent lead surely to advantage, but everyone who is hasty comes surely to poverty" (Proverbs 21:5, NASB).

B iblical leaders are committed to personal planning which is centered around God's plan for your life. The plan is guided by the wisdom of God's Word and wise counselors. These key verses give hope to the planning process:

> *"Thy word is a lamp unto my feet, and a light unto my path"*
> *(Psalm 119:105, KJV).*

> *"'For I know the plans I have for you,' declares the Lord, 'plans*
> *to prosper you and not to harm you, plans to give you hope and a*
> *future'" (Jeremiah 29:11, KJV).*

Leaders must be prepared for the leadership journey. There will be good days and bad days. There will be circumstances that seem uncontrollable, but the best leaders are the ones that are prepared.

Leadership preparation includes the following:

Cognitive Development: knowing your subject so well that you become an expert.

Competency Development: learning to be the best in your field through study and its wise application. Competency is gained by taking knowledge and applying it to the situations of life — that application is called wisdom. For Christian leaders, this wisdom always flows from the source of wisdom which is the Word of God. Wisdom can be gained through prayer and obedience to the voice of the Holy Spirit. Are you a competent leader?

Character Development: allowing God to shape one's character into the likeness of Christ.

Someone said, "Those who fail to plan, plan to fail." I am convinced that you cannot be a successful leader unless you are prepared. Over the years, as I've taught graduate students, I've required every student to write out ten life goals. I also required a personal life mission statement from each student. Why? Because current research tells us that 87% of today's population are life-takers. They accept life every day but have no ambitions, plans, or dreams. Ten percent of the population will be life-planners. They dream, think, and plan but never take action to initiate the plans. Three percent of the population will be prepared leaders.

Leaders, will you be prepared?

Day 9

Leaders Strive for the Highest Calling

"Brethren, I count not myself to have apprehended: but this one thing I do, forgetting those things which are behind, and reaching forth unto those things which are before, I press toward the mark for the prize of the high calling of God in Christ Jesus" (Philippians 3:13-14, KJV).

Biblical leaders change history. They are not content with mediocrity. Martin Luther, a German theologian, brought about the Protestant Reformation with his challenge to the church. He believed that we should be able to communicate with God and search the truth of Scripture. God used Martin Luther to proclaim that salvation is by faith alone. Wow! He changed history. An uneducated Dwight L. Moody challenged the wickedness of the day in Chicago and through his preaching turned the hearts of the people of that city toward God. His ministry expanded far and wide and historians suggest that Moody eventually led more than five million people to salvation.

How do leaders strive for the High Calling?

Leaders forget past failures and struggles. We cannot dwell on what we did poorly in the past and be successful. Satan loves this tool more than any other. Leaders must move forward toward the prize.

Leaders focus all their energy and effort on doing their best for the Kingdom. The words "reaching forth" convey putting forth every effort, straining with all that is within to accomplish a goal. This is only accomplished through living in the power of the Holy Spirit. Every great leader leaves it all on the playing field in order to accomplish success. Are you striving and giving all?

The focus is upon Christ. The focus is on having the mind of Christ. The focus is on growing and maturing to accomplish the worthwhile goal of the ultimate prize of being with Christ.

Leadership is about stepping out into the deep water. Anyone can be critical of others. Anyone can fit in and go with the flow. But will you become a disrupter for the prize of the high calling?

Leaders, let's get practical. You will never be a leader if you do not lead.

Day 10

Leaders are Accountable

"Listen carefully to my wisdom; take to heart what I can teach you. You'll treasure its sweetness deep within; you'll give it bold expression in your speech. To make sure your foundation is trust in God, I'm laying it all out right now just for you. I'm giving you thirty sterling principles — tested guidelines to live by. Believe me — these are truths that work, and will keep you accountable to those who sent you" (Proverbs 22:17-21, MSG).

Biblical leaders are accountable. The basis of this accountability comes from the fact that we must all give an account to God for our lives. From a practical standpoint, leaders are only successful when accomplishing the plans that are set forth for the organization. Once a plan has been determined, it must be integrated into the daily work of the individual, group or organization. The focus changes from what is hoped for or intended to what gets done.

Benjamin Franklin wrote, "Well done is better than well said." An effective plan is one that produces intended results. The plan is not "operationalized" until the goals are met.

It is one thing to say you intend to do something and quite another to actually do it. Eddie Rickenbacker said, "I can give you a six-word formula for success: Think things through, then follow through." It is during implementation that the most difficult work begins.

Accountability occurs when the core values, vision, mission, strategic goals, and action steps are clearly understood and shared among all stakeholders. The stakeholder team then overcomes resistance and obstacles to ensure mission accomplished. It is during the implementation stage that little things are done well and attention to detail matters.

Biblical leaders are accountable to God, their boards, and the organization and people they serve.

Leaders, are you being accountable?

Day 11

Leaders Grow in the Word

"Thy word is a lamp unto my feet, and a light unto my path"
(Psalm 119:105, KJV).

Biblical leaders understand that God's Word is truth. It is the authority for our lives. A leader must know the only true foundation is the Word. I have found the Word guides my thoughts and actions in the organizations I lead. As leaders, we should follow the example of Peter and John in Acts 2 and live the Word with boldness. Dr. Tom Arington, who is known as 'Mr. Generic Drug' for developing processes to lower costs for the industry, has led several companies and is chairman of Prasco Laboratories. He boldly displays Bibles and teaches the Word to his employees whether he is leading a public or private company. One of my heroes, Dr. Allan Brown, an Old Testament scholar, says the following about the value of the Word.

The Word:

Produces growth – *"As newborn babes desire the sincere milk of the Word that ye may grow…"(I Peter 2:2, KJV).*

Builds defense – *"Put on the whole armour of God…"*
(Ephesians 6:11-17, KJV). The Word girds our loins with truth.

Sheds light – *"The entrance of thy word giveth light..."* (*Psalm 119:105, KJV*). It guides through the darkness and keeps us on the path.

Brings freedom – *"...thy word is truth"(John 17:17, KJV)*; *"And ye shall know the truth, and the truth shall make you free"* (*John 8:32, KJV*). Truth is liberating.

Produces faith – *"So then faith cometh by hearing and hearing by the word of God"* (*Romans 10:17, KJV*).

Convicts the spirit – *"For the word of God is quick and powerful and sharper than any two-edged sword piercing even to the dividing asunder of soul and spirit..."* (*Hebrews 4:12, KJV*).

Converts the soul – *"The law of the Lord is perfect, converting the soul"* (*Psalm 19:7, KJV*).

Cleanses the heart – *"Now ye are clean through the word..."* (*John 15:3, KJV*); *"Having therefore these promises...let us cleanse ourselves from all filthiness..."* (*II Corinthians 7:1, KJV*); *"Wherewithal shall a young man cleanse his way? By taking heed to the word"* (*Psalm 119:9, KJV*).

Corrects – *"All scripture is given by inspiration of God and is profitable for doctrine, for reproof, for correction, for instruction in righteousness"* (*II Timothy 3:16, KJV*).

Brings comfort – *"Wherefore comfort one another with these words..."* (*I Thessalonians 4:18, KJV*).

Brings a crown – *"Blessed are they that do his commandments that they may have the right to the tree of life"* (*Revelation 22:14, KJV*).

Leaders, grow in the Word!

Day 12

Leaders Embrace Change

"Have I not commanded you? Be strong and courageous!
Do not tremble or be dismayed, for the Lord your God
is with you wherever you go" (Joshua 1:9, NASB).

Leaders embrace change. They take the initiative to confront and conquer any issues that diminish the well-being of their followers or interfere with their appropriate quality of life. By their words and actions, leaders help others change their world, and they help to preserve order in the midst of change.

The influence that leaders have on the world is based largely on a willingness to expand their vision. They are not afraid to go into the unknown and say, as Caleb, the Old Testament leader, *"...give me this mountain..." (Joshua 14:12, NKJV)*. Leaders see the giants in the land as an opportunity, not as a threat.

How do we embrace and understand change? In *Leading Change*, John Kotter identifies several characteristics of effective change. Among these are:

Necessity – In order to maintain a competitive edge, organizations and individuals must see that change is necessary.

Urgency – If change is to occur, a sense of urgency must propel
the individual or company to action.

Vision – Vision molds and clarifies the need for change and assists
in structuring implementation.

Communication – Communication translates the vision and enables
it to take effect.

Teamwork – Change is best realized when individual talents and
strengths are combined.

To be successful, leaders, people, organizations, businesses, schools,
government, faith-based or nonprofit institutions must each develop
a plan to deal with the reality of accelerated cultural change. Since
biblical leaders know that the foundation is sure in the Word of God,
they must think more clearly, work smarter, dream bigger, and reach
higher to Know Him and to make Him Known.

On an individual basis we must ask:

In what ways am I operating from a fearful point of view?

How does this limit my ability to influence my world in a positive way?

If I am to lead effectively, how and what must I change?

The challenge for today is for all of us to be a Joshua and a Caleb.
Leaders, we must take the land — leading and embracing change while
resting on our firm foundation.

Day 13

Leaders are Faithful

"The king said to me, 'What is it you want?' Then I prayed to the God of heaven, and I answered the king, 'If it pleases the king and if your servant has found favor in his sight, let him send me to the city in Judah where my ancestors are buried so that I can rebuild it.' Then the king, with the queen sitting beside him, asked me, 'How long will your journey take, and when will you get back?' It pleased the king to send me; so I set a time" (Nehemiah 2:4-6).

One of my favorite characters in the Bible is Nehemiah. This man gained the trust of the king because of his faithful service. Now think with me, this is not common — the king relied on a foreigner to taste his food and wine — the most trusted man in the kingdom was the cupbearer. The life of the king was in his hands. Day after day Nehemiah built trust with the king by faithfully doing his job. The king trusted Nehemiah so much that he gave him whatever he desired. In this case it resulted in the wall being rebuilt in Jerusalem.

The king's chief concern was, "Nehemiah, when will you be back?" The king counted on this guy! Here is the beauty of this story: Nehemiah was so faithful that he organized, led, and finished the wall project in fifty-two days. Now, I have seen that wall; that was no small task. This man was a leader that went above and beyond.

Leaders, are you faithful in the day-to-day? While I was serving in a low-level administrative position, one of my bosses said, "Mark, you will keep moving up the leadership ladder because you always do what you say you will do." I just call it being faithful.

God has been so kind in allowing me to raise many millions of dollars for His kingdom. Recently someone asked me, "How do you raise so much money?"

I was quickly reminded that money is only raised when people trust that you are being faithful and trustworthy. For thirty years I have connected to people daily, kept every telephone number, asked for business cards, served others, and now they know I am a faithful servant so they give to the causes that God has entrusted me to lead. It does not happen overnight.

Be faithful, dear leaders, and watch God multiply your efforts.

Day 14

Leaders Seize the Moment

"Therefore be careful how you walk, not as unwise men but as wise, making the most of your time, because the days are evil. So then do not be foolish, but understand what the will of the Lord is" (Ephesians 5: 15-17, NASB).

What does it mean for a leader to seize the moment? Opportunity is often fleeting. In fact, we are reminded as leaders in 2 Corinthians 6:2, *"Now is the day of salvation."* Spiritually speaking, all of us must be aware of the Holy Spirit convicting us of sin in our lives and all of us must accept the gracious gift of salvation. This is where we must start personally. Have you accepted Christ into your life?

As leaders there are also opportunities for the organization. How do we seize those opportunities?

First, to lead above and beyond, a leader must be keenly aware of his/her environment. Leaders often see opportunities where others do not. Leaders see further and see more than the average person. Leaders, be aware of opportunity matches. In other words, get out of your office and into your communities so you know what is happening.

Second, to see opportunities, a leader must be open to new ideas. Often I hear ideas that seem far-fetched, but every time I open my mind to really listen to others, I learn. Some of the best ideas seem to be the most ridiculous at first glance, but through thoughtful planning, these ideas become organization-movers. What new ideas are you hearing?

Third, a leader must make connections with those who can help offer insight into the opportunities being presented, and with people who have knowledge and expertise in new areas being considered. Leaders must constantly surround themselves with experts on many topics to facilitate growth and opportunities. I have learned that an expert in almost any subject is only a phone call away if I have been out connecting and listening. Create a file of these individuals so you may readily tap their expertise when needed.

Fourth, a leader must seize opportunities, and be willing and courageous enough to move forward on projects. Perhaps the most difficult aspect of seizing the moment is having the courage to move quickly on opportunities. Opportunities are fleeting and often one must make decisions quickly in this technology-filled world. It takes courage to step out and help lead a community. It takes courage to lead a church or business, but we must seize the moment. With each new opportunity and new idea, use the anchor of prayer as the guiding decision-maker in your life.

Leaders, let's seize the moment.

Day 15

Leaders are Servants

"For even the Son of Man came not to be served but to serve others and to give his life as a ransom for many" (Matthew 20:28, NLT).

Biblical leaders serve. The most important gift leaders can give to an organization is to serve the team. Leaders are not leaders unless they have followers, and leaders must serve their followers. Jesus Christ gives the ultimate example of servant leadership; He served all of His followers on many occasions. He then gave His life for others. That is servant leadership!

Dr. Jim Laub defines servant leadership as "an understanding and practice of leadership that places the good of those led over the self-interest of the leader." Laub describes effective servant leaders as those who:

Display Authenticity – Servant leadership begins with a different view of yourself as leader. You are to be open, real, approachable, and accountable to others. You are not higher than others due to your 'position.' In fact, position speaks to responsibility, not value. As you work with people within organizations, you will serve them if you display the quality of authenticity.

Value People – Servant leadership requires a different view of others. People are to be valued and developed, not used for the purposes of the leader. As a leader, I accept the fact that people have present value, not just future potential. People seem to have an innate ability to know whether or not they are being valued — whether or not they are being trusted. As servants we accept a person's value up front. We give them the gift of trust without requiring that they earn it first. As you work with individuals in organizations, you will serve them if you display the quality of valuing people.

Develop People – As servants, we view others differently. Part of my responsibility is to help others grow toward their potential as servants and leaders. Therefore, I am looking to create a dynamic learning environment that encourages growth and development. As I interact with others, I am conscious of what we are learning together. The mistakes of others are opportunities to learn. We know that people have both present value and future potential. As you work with people within organizations, you will serve them if you display the quality of developing people.

As leaders our goal must always be to serve.

Leaders, are you leading by serving?

Day 16

Women Go Lead!

"Go, gather together all the Jews that are present in Shushan, and fast ye for me, and neither eat nor drink three days, night or day: I also and my maidens will fast likewise; and so will I go in unto the king, which is not according to the law: and if I perish, I perish" (Esther 4:16, KJV).

The biblical character, Esther, is a great example of servant leadership. She showed great courage by placing her life on the line for her people. Sound familiar? Jesus did that for us. Leaders' confidence is in Christ, not themselves. Their passion for others and for their organization's success supersedes their personal desires and fears. They are on their knees in prayer in order to courageously stand strong. Esther first appears as an orphan, but, as Edith Deen points out, "Four years later she rises to the position of a queen with amazing power, a power which she manages wisely."

Despite her humble beginnings, Esther was placed in a leadership role and was then able to become God's tool to save the Jewish population from extermination. Deen highlights the leadership strategies that Esther modeled in leading the Jews out of harm's way:

She gained favor with the people.

She used sound judgment.

She thought of others first.
She offered to sacrifice her position and even her life to save others.
She was dedicated and loyal.
She exhibited virtuous character.
She was fearless.
She was prudent.

Esther's life offers a pattern that each of us can follow. Could it be that the characteristics listed above might resolve the situation you so desire to change? You can be that leader. Women go lead!

One of the greatest problems in our world today is the lack of leadership. Many are afraid to share great ideas with their organizations or ministries. They do not lead. To the leaders of companies, listen up: Great leaders empower others by encouraging them to positively present creative ideas without presumption in order to improve the organization. The front line has those ideas. Go, ask, and listen.

The reasons employees do not lead are as follows: some are afraid; some do not have favor; some have poor work habits; some do not believe their ideas are valuable or valued; and some do not care. Even more tragically, many leaders are too controlling, too close-minded, or too indifferent to care what their employees think.

Esther changed her world. Which of Esther's leadership strategies might work for you?

Leaders, go lead!

Day 17

Leaders Overcome Obstacles

"What shall we then say to these things?
If God be for us, who can be against us?" (Romans 8:31, KJV)

For every obstacle there is a way —
over, under, around, or through.
So when you have begun a good project,
'Never, Never, Never Quit.'
— attributed to Sir Winston Churchill

Leaders, have the attitude of Churchill and the biblical character, Joshua! They would not quit.

Joshua challenges me as a leader. Have you ever studied his life? What a leader! His motto was "Giants — what giants? Have you met my God?" Joshua saw God, and he saw the promised land, but everyone else saw the obstacles. Which do you see when new vision is before you, obstacles or the promised land?

I wanted to be a Christian university administrator. So, between the ages of twenty and thirty, I completed all the degree requirements for Associates, Bachelors, Masters and Doctorate — well, almost! Then I was in a car accident three months before my last two chapters of dissertation were edited and revised. Oh no! Not this, God! I am finished. But then I corrected my God-view. Do you take time to think and pray about your view of God? Months in bed, multiple surgeries, and learning to walk again would not deter me from that accurate God-view. I must add that God gave me a wife who beautifully helped me edit and revise my dissertation (she says she earned her doctorate also!) and it was finally completed. Obstacles did not block the course of history for my life.

If I had not gotten the doctorate, my life and so many students' lives would not be changed. Thank God for the right view.

So, what is your perspective? "The giants are so big. There are giants as far as I can see!" Do you ever think, "What are the legal issues for this ministry?" or, "If we only had personnel?" or, "Have we already lost this battle?" Or "Is the government giant too big?" As leaders, you must find and focus on God's view.

Doubters say, "We are so small and there are so many of them. Wow! How can we make an impact?"

Leaders, I challenge you to overcome obstacles. Get the God-view right! Be a Joshua and lead!

Day 18

Leaders Overcome Critics

"But Caleb tried to quiet the people as they stood before Moses. 'Let's go at once to take the land,' he said. 'We can certainly conquer it!' But the other men who had explored the land with him disagreed. 'We can't go up against them!'" (Numbers 13:30-31, NLT)

Leaders will always have critics. The very essence of leadership involves stepping out and setting new directions. Leaders are not leaders unless they are reaching for new territories and charting a new course. Managers maintain, but leaders see further and reach higher. They see the 'promised land.'

As Joshua and Caleb viewed the land for forty days with ten other spies, they were the only ones with the right vision — a God vision.

Critics saw the size of the enemy. Joshua remembered the significance of his God. Critics saw all the battles yet to fight. Joshua focused on the promised land.

I had the privilege of leading an organization during a period of exceptional growth. During that period of time, critics were always not far behind. Their words still ring: "He is so young," "He is not missional," "He is moving too fast," "That is against policy," "We tried that already," "That is too big for us." These are the same giants we face today.

At these times we need a new God-view! Joshua and Caleb stood up to the critics. Leaders have courage. The source of your strength is from above. Keep your eyes on the promised land. Do not focus on the critics.

We faced attacks by critics as we were working to build that organization, but God helped us to never lose focus. The organization grew because we overcame the critics.

Criticism will destroy a leader unless his focus is on God. Do you want to go on a journey of growth? Stay Focused. Overcome the critics! Build a team of visionary people who cling to God's promises. And if you are a critic, be careful, you may just be opposing a God-move.

Don't blame Joshua — be a leader!

Day 19

Leaders Don't Take Shortcuts

"'...Therefore I felt compelled, and offered a burnt offering.' And Samuel said to Saul, 'You have done foolishly. You have not kept the commandment of the Lord your God, which He commanded you. For now the Lord would have established your kingdom over Israel forever. But now your kingdom shall not continue. The Lord has sought for Himself a man after His own heart, and the Lord has commanded him to be commander over His people, because you have not kept what the Lord commanded you'" (I Samuel 13:12-14, NKJV).

Leaders must not take shortcuts. Some time ago, my family and I were headed to a small town in Tennessee. I knew the way and always took the interstate so everything was fine. On this occasion, I got an idea for a shortcut. I saw on the map that if I took a side road I could cut off about 100 miles. On the map, the road looked great so I turned off the exit and started on the shortcut. My first clue should have been that the road significantly narrowed a couple of miles away from the interstate. Another warning should have been the unmarked roads. The further we traveled, the more curves and hills appeared. What a shortcut — several hours later, after a few stops for directions, we arrived at our destination. The shortcut had been a major detour.

This story reminds me of two classics. In "The Wizard of Oz", Dorothy, Scarecrow, Tin Man, and the Lion were sidetracked by taking a shortcut. Christian, in "Pilgrims Progress", was also sidetracked by shortcuts.

Leaders must remember that shortcuts in our personal moral lives will destroy our organizations. Shortcuts destroy God's plan.

Here are some biblical examples:

Abraham had a promise to be father of the nation of Israel, but he did it his way and brought much suffering to his life and the nation. God's design was for Abraham and Sarah to birth the nation of Israel, but Hagar the Egyptian handmaiden was used to conceive a child. Abraham and Sarah suffered as both took shortcuts.

In dealing with his brother Jacob, Esau took a shortcut. As a result, Esau lost his birthright.

How many shortcuts did Saul take? Saul was told to wait until Samuel arrived, but he offered the sacrifice himself and lost the favor of God.

Shortcuts produce consequences that are swift, serious and significant. Leaders, think with me. Where are you taking shortcuts? Below are only a few possible consequences:

Sexual immorality – disease, unwanted pregnancy, families destroyed, children heartbroken, scars for life.

Lying – guilty conscience, person destroyed, organization hurt, permanent damage when discovered.

Leaders, please do not take shortcuts. Be persons of character.

Day 20

Leaders are Visionary

"Where there is no vision, the people perish"
(Proverbs 29:18, KJV).

My first pastorate was in a small country church. They were great people but they needed vision. The church had dwindled from 150 down to 25 in attendance. When we arrived, we sensed God telling us to grow the church. We presented that vision each month and God began to bless. The church doubled that year and continued five straight years of growth. During that time, I learned something about vision — without vision an organization will not move forward. Leaders should be visionaries.

The difference between a leader and a manager is vision. Leaders present new vision while managers implement vision. What exactly is vision? Bennis and Nanus define it as, "a mental image of a possible and desirable future state of the organization." George Barna agrees when referring to ministry-related vision by suggesting that "vision for ministry is a clear mental image of a preferable future imparted by God."

Most broad-based definitions of vision include these key elements:

Vision defines the future.

Vision is purpose-driven.

Vision crystallizes creative thought.

Vision sets direction and promotes action.

Vision uses wisdom from the past.

Vision reaches for the impossible.

Vision becomes reality when conceptualized.

Vision must be communicated.

Vision must be shared to overcome hindrances.

When Nehemiah had a vision to build the wall, he shared it with the people. The people had a mind to work and God blessed the effort. A wall was built around the city of Jerusalem. Leaders, do you have vision for the future?

Leaders who move organizations from status quo to status go will constantly be thinking about the future. They will dream dreams and have visions. They will see farther and reach higher for their team.

Leaders, what is your vision for your organization?

Day 21

Biblical Leaders
Believe in Prayer and Faith

*"And whatever you ask in My name, that I will do,
that the Father may be glorified in the Son" (John 14:13, NKJV).*

God has taught me about prayer and faith in my leadership journey. My first experience was as a 13- or 14-year-old young man. I was asked by my grandmother to raise the family pig. My dad also bought a pig to grow for our family. This was my first business venture, so I invested fifty dollars and was excited about having extra cash that fall. As the summer passed, my pig would not grow and was almost fifty pounds lighter than the other pig. I examined it and discovered that it had developed a hernia. I decided to pray for that pig, and so I anointed the pig with mom's cooking oil and prayed that God would touch it. Do you think God heard the prayers of a young man? Yes, he did. That pig began to grow and nearly caught up to the other pig. I know what you're thinking and, yes, I can sell you some of that oil. Seriously — Wow! My God-view changed.

In our first pastorate, Debbie and I watched as God built our faith when we pledged the first $1,000 for a church building project. We were only making $75 dollars per week after taxes. Yet, He supplied our need to pay that pledge and in that time, when we had little, God added another blessing. One of His servants gave us money for our anniversary dinner and a night away. Wow! God sometimes blows our minds. Prayer and faith work. God has a way of showing His love so graciously. By the way, in three years, the church was built and paid for — because God gave the vision.

These small incidents built my faith and caused me to ask God for bigger things. Vision had been expanded, and so I asked God for more.

Leaders, do you have big vision? How is your prayer life? Do you have faith? Take a step into the water and activate your faith.

Over the years I have thought of these faith-building moments so many times. It is all about your view of God.

Leaders, what is your God-view?

Day 22

Biblical Leaders Are Merciful

"Blessed are the merciful: for they shall obtain mercy" (Matthew 5:7, NKJV).

Biblical leaders are merciful because they have been given mercy. God, who was selfless, other-oriented, in one act of mercy, sent Jesus Christ as a sacrifice for our sins. In other words, it cost God His very own Son to show us mercy.

Here are a few supporting verses:

Ephesians 2:4 reminds us that God is rich in mercy: *"But God, who is rich in mercy, because of His great love with which He loved us..."*

Psalm 103:17 shares that His mercy is eternal: *"But the mercy of the Lord is from everlasting to everlasting on those who fear Him, and His righteousness to children's children."*

2 Corinthians 1:3 refers to God as the Father of mercy: *"Blessed be the God and Father of our Lord Jesus Christ, the Father of mercies and God of all comfort."*

As leaders we must ask ourselves the following questions.

How do we respond to the oppression of the downtrodden, drunkards, drug addicts, the homeless, the less fortunate?

How do we respond to the shortcomings of our brothers and sisters in the faith?

Do we want to hear all the juicy details, or is our heart smitten with mercy? John Wesley said, "I am so far from lightly believing what one man says against another, that I will not easily believe what a man says against himself."

Do we extend that mercy to others?

How tender is your heart? Is it strong, hard, insensitive, calloused?

As you hunger after God, your heart becomes tender.

Are you broken, do you shed tears?

Do you have pity for those around you who are hell-bound and hurting?

Mercy is having a tender heart.

This is a real story drawn from my leadership journey:

It started as a normal school day, with the bouncing of a basketball, loud noises, rushed goodbyes and parents scurrying off to work. And then I saw her. I had seen her many times and wondered what was behind those veiled eyes. She always looked as if she were in another world. This morning she seemed especially distraught. She stumbled through the doorway, unloaded her book bag and softly began to cry.

As an educator leader, I thought I was trained for these situations. I could handle this one. After all, every student has problems. Any principal can hurriedly reassure, brush aside, and continue on with the real academic concerns of an education.

I walked over to the scared young face. Seventeen. I thought back to the wonderful years those had been for me in my secure, traditional, two-parent home. I had cookies after school from Mom, and basketball, football, or baseball with Dad. I felt loved each day. What a wonderful life!

But her situation was different. She had two dads, lived in the poorest area in town, and had a brother who had been arrested for drugs. She lived with that every day, so why was she crying? The words poured from her mouth before I could ask — "Mr. Smith," she said, "I'm pregnant."

My mind began to race. Excuse me? What did you say? Did you know you are in one of the finest Christian schools in America? Did you miss the chapter on chastity? Did you not understand the rules of this school? Did you forget the last several years of biblical instruction? Then God reminded me of the woman caught in adultery in John 8, and I knew I was reacting to her hurting need in a harmful way, even perhaps being pharisaical, righteous, and proud.

Then my mind zoned in on that famous question, "What would Jesus do?" When people were abused, Jesus came to their rescue. Whether they were bruised, battered, or disappointed with life, unloved, discouraged, or helpless — Jesus wasn't concerned about His own well-being, His fame, His reputation or just plain getting dirty. Jesus showed mercy. He came to bring hope to a hurting world.

After the initial shock, common sense and the love of Christ reached through me. She talked; I listened. She cried; I cared. She prayed; we both repented, and Jesus showed us both mercy.

Leaders, show mercy.

Day 23

Biblical Leaders are Involved in World Evangelism

"And he said unto them, 'Go ye into all the world, and preach the gospel to every creature'" (Mark 16:15, KJV).

Biblical leaders are people who share in the mission of Christ. Jesus came to minister, to touch the lost and lonely, to lift the downtrodden and despised, to give hope to the sad and the sin-sick. He was here for those who need a Savior; there was no other purpose.

God created Adam and Eve in His image. He made them with a free will which allowed them to obey or disobey. We all know how that turned out. When Satan entered the picture and tempted Adam and Eve to disobey God's only commandment, they began a life of sin and misery.

God wanted to restore a right relationship with this man and woman He created. His ultimate plan was to send His Son, Jesus Christ, to pay the penalty for our sins by dying on the cross in our place. Even though the plan was carried out over 2,000 years ago, we are reminded of it when we hear it put to music, "When He was on the cross, I was on His mind" (Ronnie Hinson).

"But God demonstrates his own love for us in this: While we were still sinners, Christ died for us" (Romans 5:8). It is through God's love that this plan was made. It is through His plan that the metamorphic transformation is possible.

Leaders, we may try to say many things about the mission of Jesus, but He came to accomplish a divine purpose — the purpose of the Father — which was to save our ungodly souls. He came to change our lives, and in doing so, He changed the world.

So how is the mission accomplished? Each one must tell one. At first, only a small group from diverse backgrounds listened to what Jesus said, never fully realizing the mission. Somehow the message touched first one heart (maybe Peter's), and another, and then others as the gospel began to spread. Like the power within an avalanche, it gathered force and the explosion can still be felt around the world as the gospel penetrates the hearts of men and women, boys and girls, and makes them new creatures in Christ Jesus.

Friends, jump on the bandwagon of this glorious gospel; it is the only force that can change the world. Share the news, ring loud the clarion call from the hilltops, wave the banners and shout His praises. Jesus saves, Jesus saves, and He is changing the world.

Day 24

Leaders Connect with People of Influence

"A man that hath friends must shew himself friendly: and there is a friend that sticketh closer than a brother" (Proverbs 18:24, KJV).

Leaders are connectors; they quickly learn that nothing is accomplished in life without friends. I heard the number one leadership expert, Dr. John Maxwell, share that one of the secrets to success in leadership is the arena of connecting.

Leaders must connect to persons outside their own life and/or organization. This requires a purposeful plan of who, where, and what you want to learn — and then connection.

One of the keys to life is to connect with influencers. While serving as an administrator for the last twenty-plus years, I have connected with politicians, educational leaders, business leaders, corporate executives, pastoral and mission leaders. I have learned from the best. Not only has this broadened my thought process, but the growth has exponentially expanded my influence. Leaders who want to impact society must connect to every level of society. In other words, you must be friendly in order to have friends.

One powerful practice is to do the following for biblical influence:

Collect the name and number of every influencer.

Write a note about each person so you remember key facts about them. Write, call or text them occasionally to stay connected.

Who are the connectors you need to know to move your church or organization forward? Write down five names today, and connect with them within one month.

Attend conferences, go where leaders are, make calls, and show up at events or at their offices to ensure that you will be connected.

What are you doing to connect? Never forget that connectors are only successful if they share their connections. Value added is always in direct proportion to the value you add and share. Don't forget to share connections!

This is not a secret exam; it is an explosion of momentum for the sake of the Kingdom. Connections lead to influence, which allows these networks to accomplish major initiatives with you. Life is about connections. I call them God connections.

Leaders, are you investing in connections? Leadership is about connections. Connect and change the world.

Day 25

Leaders Develop Leaders and Multiply Vision

"For I will look on you favorably and make you fruitful, multiply you and confirm My covenant with you" (Leviticus 26:9, NKJV).

Leadership is about investing in people. One of the greatest lessons I have learned is the high value of working with others to grow an organization. In my younger years, it was all too easy to roll up my sleeves and try to accomplish the vision whether others followed or not. After a few years, I became keenly aware that, on my own, growth only occurs by addition, but real growth comes through multiplication.

Multiplicational growth happens when the leader engages team members to develop and accomplish the vision. Leaders, whether you're working with volunteers or full-time employees, the organization will not move into a multiplication stage without the leader developing more leaders and turning them loose to serve. Develop leaders — let go — and see what happens. Some of the leaders will fail, which will aid in their development. Those moments will be teachable moments in which you can invest heavily. I have learned that people have value, and we should not easily allow failure to destroy them.

Still other leaders will flourish and learn by osmosis. They will take every word you suggest and learn and grow far beyond what you can imagine. Whatever method is used, leaders will be developed.

What is your plan to develop leaders for multiplication?

In my first pastorate, I only had three or four leaders with whom I could spend much time to expand the vision of the church. There were only two or three men in the church, but one man caught a vision for a men's ministry, and within a year, eighteen to twenty men were part of the men's group. The men's group started a ministry that served the elderly once a month on Saturday mornings. They shoveled coal, painted, and did yard work for donations. The donations led to a church being built in a remote village in Mexico. One man had a vision and two churches were built.

This one man showed me much about leadership through this lesson on multiplication. Since then, I have led hundreds of people in large organizations, but have always remembered the multiplication principle.

This multiplication principle was used by Christ to reach the world. One man worked with twelve others and the world has forever been changed through His message of salvation.

Leaders, who are you developing? Get busy!

Day 26

Leaders Build Great Board Relations

"Now we ask you, brothers, to respect those who work hard among you, who are over you in the Lord and who admonish you. Hold them in the highest regard in love because of their work. Live in peace with each other" (1 Thessalonians 5:12,13).

Many leaders go into board meetings with fear and trepidation. They view the board in an adversarial way and as a place of confrontation. Here are tips that will change the way you view the board:

Leaders must look for wisdom. A board is a place of counsel. *"Plans fail for lack of counsel, but with many advisers they succeed" (Proverbs 15:22).*

At times leaders have board members who vociferously oppose their direction, but leaders who keep their spirits open to even their worst critics will find nuggets of gold. It is amazing how much one can learn when evaluating what every person is saying. A correct view of the wisdom of the board yields dividends in many ways.

Leaders work with boards on policy and strategy, not day-to-day management. Over the years I have watched many organizations flounder because they discussed the "electric bill" instead of strategies to reach a world for Christ.

Leaders, elevate the agenda! As leaders, you must be prepared to lead the agenda and elevate the meeting. Leaders must know where meetings are going, whether at a small church or on a university board. Effective leaders think through all scenarios, learn board members' agendas through private chats beforehand, and build the agenda to accommodate board members' desires or concerns while still leading. At the same time, leaders must always work to elevate meetings from personal differences to the substance of the issue at hand. Leaders must work together to solve problems.

Leaders, do you plan and elevate your board meetings above the mundane?

I have learned that board members are wise counselors to leadership. As leaders, you must find a way to move the organization forward through working and elevating those around you to an agenda that will impact the world.

Leaders, be status go, not status quo! Lead, my friends, above and beyond.

Day 27

Leaders Give an Account, Focus and Follow Through

"So then every one of us shall give account of himself to God"
(Romans 14:12, KJV).

Leaders understand accountability. It is what drives them above and beyond the norm. Many times, however, those in positions of leadership lose their way due to the complexity and quantity of issues with which they are faced while in leadership.

While serving on Ohio's State Board of Education, we were held to the highest of standards regarding accountability. Every action, perceived or not, was under public scrutiny. Additionally, while serving in ministry settings, every one of my leadership actions has been reviewed by friend and foe. Accountability has become a mainstay of my life. But as I reviewed this writing, I understood in a new way that accountability is a supremely biblical concept. My life will be reviewed by the almighty God. Every action and deed will be reviewed. Now that is accountability to the max.

President Ronald Reagan was known for saying, "Trust but verify." A leader in higher education used to say, "Inspect what you expect."

Leaders who are above and beyond always hold their teams to accountability. All leaders need to focus. If a church or business wants growth, then it must focus on creating growth opportunities with goals; but above all, accountability must be a key part of the plan.

Dr. Larry Lindsay, former director of the National Economic Council, and I have worked for many years in leadership to ensure above and beyond results. Here is a simple suggested model for your organization:

Select a goal

Select an assessment measure

List performance criteria

Collect and analyze the data

Compare to existing data

Recommend changes or improvements

Accountability to growth is shown by supporting the budgets and training necessary for the growth and requiring year-end reporting. Consider making the day you turn in these budgets a celebration day to ensure that all see the success or, in some cases, the future items to be celebrated. The difference between a good and great organization is accountability. The difference between success and failure is follow-through.

Leaders, who will ensure accountability in your organization?

Day 28

Leaders Invest in Young Leaders

"So the Lord said to Moses, 'Take Joshua the son of Nun, a man in whom is the Spirit, and lay your hand on him; and have him stand before Eleazar the priest and before all the congregation, and commission him in their sight'"
(Numbers 27: 18-19, NASB).

A key to successful leadership is to invest in the younger generation. Moses is an example for all leaders in the way that he chose his successor, Joshua. Joshua was a faithful servant to Moses and had earned the leader's trust.

Why invest in the younger generation? I have learned that they are able to bring a new energy level to the organization. As biblical leaders who go above and beyond, we should introduce them to their source of strength and energy, the Holy Spirit.

Perhaps one of the most powerful lessons I learned from my mentor and former boss, Dr. Jim Barnes, was as follows: An organization must have energy, so hire a group of "young thoroughbreds," and turn them loose. They will make mistakes, but their energy will lead the organization to a new level. Many growing organizations hire young leaders. New young leaders help the organization to avoid becoming static and stale. Organizations cannot move to a new level until fresh, young, energetic workers with new ideas are mixed in with the wise experts. The dynamism this group brings will spur an outburst of energy and result in growth.

At one of the prior places I served, I tried this strategy. I worked to bring in five to ten young couples to bring energy and dynamism. Within months I noticed the entire energy level had been lifted. The organization began to grow and hundreds of new clients were served. That organization grew tenfold due in part to a group of young, energetic leaders. They were everywhere, looking to be involved.

I have found, however, that most organizations ignore the younger generation. Leaders, don't just give them the dirty jobs; invest in them and watch them take the organization above and beyond what it has been. Let them be part of the power structure. Let them try new ideas. Believe me, it works.

I have found these strategies to be true especially for ministry:

If you love a young couple and give them responsibility, they will thankfully pour themselves into the ministry.

If you give them a voice and allow for their ideas to be tried, their energy will explode for your ministry.

If you create a safe haven for them to try and fail and are an encouragement to them, they will try new ideas.

If you set the example of a careful righteous lifestyle and teach it to them, almost all will follow.

Leaders, I dare you to save this generation by investing in young people! Do it today and make them feel wanted. Don't hold them off, but learn how to take the power of the energy in youth and direct it toward God.

Day 29

Leaders Build a Team

"Though one may be overpowered, two can defend themselves. A cord of three strands is not quickly broken" (Ecclesiastes 4:12).

W hile visiting Yosemite National Park, the great sequoia tree reminded me of a powerful leadership lesson: the power of a team. These giant trees are some of the largest trees in the world — so large that a car can pass through an opening in them with room to spare. An interesting fact our ranger shared with us is that these trees need each other to survive. Immediately, my mind went to working with teams.

There are different kinds of gifts, but the same Spirit distributes them. There are different kinds of service, but the same Lord (I Corinthians 12:4-5).

The team grows strong as each uses the gifts and abilities to strengthen the team. The Sequoia grows strong and withstands massive storms by interlocking its root system with other Sequoias. Whether in the church or your organization, the team becomes stronger by building on the strengths of each individual contributor. In the 21st century, many organizations are missing this concept. The leader cannot be autocratic, self-absorbed, or a protectionist. The leader must be about building a team. We are not in a competition; we need each other. We must learn to build on each other's gifts and abilities.

Leaders also understand that the team grows stronger through fire and testing. Studies have found that fire is required for the strengthening and growth of the giant Sequoia. In fact, it will not survive long-term if it is not introduced to fire. We hate testing, but if a team does not have to work through problems, think, and strategize, then mediocrity and complacency become part of the organization. This is why early success can be dangerous. Teams must be deep and tested in order to understand true leadership that is above and beyond. Teams typically "think" or "sink" in testing times. Effective leaders focus on building strong teams that support each other.

Will you lead your team to the growth it can enjoy? Non-leaders often do not lead because of the problems that come with growth. Who wants problems? This is a God-view I gained from the great Sequoia.

Leaders, build a team and lead your organization to success.

Day 30

Leaders Lead a Victorious Christian Life

*"But thanks be to God, which giveth us the victory through
our Lord Jesus Christ" (I Corinthians 15:57, KJV).*

Leaders who live above and beyond are victorious in many aspects of life, but it all begins with daily victorious Christian living. It is a daily process through the power of the Holy Spirit.

The first step to daily victorious living is a recognition that we are all sinners and that there is a sin problem in our world. We then recognize that humanity is unable to do anything about the problem, so we need a remedy. That remedy is found in the redemptive plan of God, the offering of His Son, Jesus Christ, as the sacrifice for sin. When we ask for forgiveness and accept this gift of salvation, a spiritual transformation occurs whereby we become children of God and partakers of the divine inheritance. Jesus becomes our Savior as we become new creations in Christ.

One may ask, what is this saving faith? Dr. Robertson McQuilkin (former president of CIU) suggested, "It is not just saying with my lips, 'I believe.' Even the devil and imps of hell believe!" According to James 2:19 it is being:

Convinced with my mind Jesus is my Savior (mind)

Convicted in my heart that He died for me (emotions)

Committed with my will to follow Christ (commitment)

This begins the life of victorious Christian living.

This victorious Christian life is also a daily surrender to the Lordship of Christ. Daily we walk in the light of His Word. The Holy Spirit living within us corrects, reproves, rebukes, and guides this beautiful life and keeps us in tune with the life of Christ. If we stumble and fall, we are quick to repent and follow after Christ with all of our hearts.

Romans 12: 1-2 reminds us of this life by saying God wants all of who we are.

"There, I urge you, brothers and sisters, in view of God's mercy, to offer your bodies as a living sacrifice, holy and pleasing to God — this is your true and proper worship. Do not conform to the pattern of this world, but be transformed by the renewing of your mind. Then you will be able to test and approve what God's will is — His good, pleasing and perfect will" *(Romans 12:1-2).*

Lastly, this victorious Christian life is lived out in a life of service, following Christ's example.

"For even the Son of Man did not come to be served, but to serve, and to give His life as a ransom for many" *(Mark 10:45).*

"In your relationships with one another, have the same mindset as Christ Jesus who, being in very nature God, did not consider equality with God something to be used to His own advantage; rather, He made himself nothing by taking the very nature of a servant, being made in human likeness" *(Philippians 2:5-7).*

Leaders, you were not created for self, you were created to serve.

About the Author

With over two decades of experience in leadership roles, Dr. Mark A. Smith, president of Columbia International University, has committed his life to the advancement of the gospel through Christian higher education. He comes to CIU from Ohio Christian University where he served as president for eleven years and grew enrollment from 400 to 4,600 students. Before that, he held the role of vice president of graduate studies at Indiana Wesleyan University and oversaw the doubling of its enrollment from approximately 5,000 to 10,000 students. Dr. Smith led a growing church as senior Pastor and lives out his passion for leadership every day. Dr. Smith has co-authored several books on practical leadership including *Leading Change* which has sold over 250,000 copies. He shares his timeless insights in this guide.

CIU | Columbia International University

Columbia International University has taken its place among the leading Christian universities and seminaries in America as we adapt with time and technology while staying true to our mission: CIU educates students from a biblical worldview to impact the nations with the message of Christ.

For more information about undergraduate, graduate, and seminary programs at Columbia International University, visit
www.ciu.edu

Made in the USA
Columbia, SC
24 April 2019